Jordan

A

Pocket

Travel guide 2023

Exploring Jordan's Natural Wonders and Discovering the History and Culture of Amman

DANIEL C. FLICK

2 | *Jordan: a pocket travel guide*

Copyrighted material

Copyright©2023(Daniel c. Flick)

All intellectual property rights are retained. Without the express written permission of the publisher, no part of this book may be reproduced or transmitted in any form or by any means, electronic or mechanical, including photocopying, recording, or any information storing and retrieval system.

Table of Content

INTRODUCTION — 7
WHY VISIT JORDAN? — 8

CHAPTER ONE — 11

ABOUT JORDAN — 11
HISTORY OF JORDAN — 11
THE GEOGRAPHY AND CLIMATE OF JORDAN — 13

CHAPTER TWO — 15

PLANNING YOUR TRIP — 15
WHEN TO GO — 15
HOW TO GET THERE — 17
GETTING AROUND — 19
VISAS AND DOCUMENTS — 21
TRAVEL INSURANCE — 23
BUDGETING AND MONEY — 26

CHAPTER THREE — 29

ACCOMMODATIONS OPTIONS — 29
TYPES OF ACCOMMODATION — 29
BOOKING RECOMMENDATIONS — 31
RECOMMENDATIONS FOR ACCOMMODATIONS — 33

CHAPTER FOUR — 36

DESTINATION GUIDES	**36**
AMMAN	**36**
TOP ATTRACTIONS	38
HIDDEN GERMS	41
ACCOMMODATION RECOMMENDATIONS	44
PETRA	**47**
TOP ATTRACTIONS	49
HIDDEN GERMS	52
RECOMMENDATIONS FOR FOOD AND DRINK	55
RECOMMENDATIONS FOR ACCOMMODATIONS	57
DEAD SEA	**60**
TOP ATTRACTIONS	62
HIDDEN GERMS	64
RECOMMENDATIONS FOR FOOD AND DRINK	66
RECOMMENDATIONS FOR ACCOMMODATIONS	67

CHAPTER FIVE	**70**
ACTIVITIES AND EXPERIENCES	**70**
ADVENTURE SPORTS	70
CULTURAL ACTIVITIES	72
FOOD AND BEVERAGES	74
EXPERIENCES WITH WILDLIFE AND NATURE	77
FESTIVALS AND SPECIAL EVENTS	79

CHAPTER SIX	**82**
PRACTICAL INFORMATION	**82**
HEALTH AND SAFETY	82
INTERNET AND COMMUNICATION	84
ETIQUETTE AND REGIONAL TRADITIONS	85
LANGUAGE GUIDE	88

CONCLUSION _____ **93**

INTRODUCTION

Jordan has unequaled natural beauty, a rich cultural heritage, and kind people. Jordan is home to a number of valuable historical structures, including Petra, the Dead Sea, and Wadi Rum, as well as therapeutic waters and magnificent landscape. Daring tourists should explore this little Middle Eastern country because it is a hidden treasure mine of experiences.

This handy book includes the must-see attractions in Jordan as well as some off-the-beaten-path hidden discoveries. We'll take you to the best locations to eat, stay, and travel. We will also give you with crucial information about regional traditions and manners, visa needs, and travel insurance.

Our travel guide promotes eco-friendly travel habits while also making the process of planning your holiday easier. We believe that it is everyone's responsibility to respect the environment and the way of life in the region. As a result, we'll provide you some tips on how to travel safely and correctly.

So, whether you're searching for adventure, history, or just to relax in the sun and eat some of the world's best cuisine, Jordan offers something for everyone. With this useful travel guide in hand, you'll be ready to visit Jordan at its best. Are you ready to explore this incredible country? Let's get the celebration started!

Why visit Jordan?

For a number of reasons visiting Jordan ought to be on everyone's travel wish list. This country has everything to offer everyone, from its fascinating history and culture to its breathtaking natural surroundings and kind hospitality. Here are just a few of the many benefits of visiting Jordan:

The ancient city of Petra, the Roman ruins at Jerash, and the biblical Mount Nebo are just a few of the most important historical and archaeological sites in Jordan. Visiting these places provides insight into the diverse population that has resided in this area as well as its rich history and culture.

Jordan is home to several stunning natural features, such as the vividly colored Wadi Rum desert, the Red Sea's glistening waves, and the lush greenery of the Dana Biosphere Reserve. These breathtaking locations provide a variety of outdoor activities, including hiking, rock climbing, swimming, and snorkeling.

Jordanian food is a delicious fusion of Middle Eastern and Mediterranean flavors, with a focus on local, seasonal ingredients. Two dishes that you must have are falafel and the delicious lamb and rice dish called mansaf.

The people of Jordan are renowned for their friendliness and delight in introducing visitors to their traditions and culture. No matter whether you choose to stay in a modest guesthouse or visit Amman's markets, you will be welcomed with kind smiles and helpful suggestions.

steady and safe: Despite being located in a volatile region, Jordan is a safe and secure country with a low crime rate and a well-developed tourism infrastructure. Visitors may explore the country with confidence knowing they are in good hands.

These are just a few of the many reasons why visiting Jordan ought to be on everyone's travel wish list. Whether you're interested in history, the environment, cuisine, or just soaking up the local culture, this country has something to offer everyone. So why wait? Start planning your trip to Jordan right now!

CHAPTER ONE
ABOUT JORDAN

HISTORY OF JORDAN

Throughout the course of Jordan's long history, several civilizations and empires have risen and fallen. The nation has been inhabited for a very long period; Paleolithic remains from that era attest to this. Over the course of millennia, Jordan has been inhabited by a wide range of peoples, including Canaanites, Edomites, Nabateans, and Romans.

In the past, Jordan served as a hub for trade and commerce, with important caravan routes passing through the region. With Petra serving as their capital, the Nabateans—known for their skill at chiseling exquisite structures out of rock—built a thriving trade empire in Jordan. After eventually defeating the Nabateans, the Romans built several important cities in the region, notably Jerash and Amman.

In the seventh century, Islam spread to Jordan, which later joined the Islamic Caliphate. Over the next few centuries, Jordan was ruled by a series of Muslim dynasties, including the Umayyads, Abbasids, and Mamluks. During this time, a number of famous mosques and other Islamic buildings were constructed all around the country.

Early in the 20th century, Jordan was a part of the Ottoman Empire, which ruled the region until the end of World War I. Upon the conclusion of the conflict, which lasted from 1920 to 1946, Jordan was included into the British Mandate of Palestine. During this time, the country made significant social and economic growth, which included building vital infrastructure like roads, schools, and hospitals.

monarch Abdullah I reigned as Jordan's first monarch after the country's 1946 declaration of independence from Great Britain. Over the next decades, Jordan saw political unrest and bloodshed, including the Arab-Israeli War in 1948 and the Black September Crisis in 1970.

In recent years, Jordan has developed into a prosperous and successful country with a strong economy and a booming tourism industry. The country is now renowned for its deep cultural heritage, stunning natural settings, and hospitable people. Jordan continues to be a Middle Eastern symbol of progress and optimism despite its stormy past and stands as a testament to the tenacity of its people.

The geography and climate of Jordan

Jordan is a Middle Eastern country with 89,342 square kilometers of land area. Saudi Arabia, Iraq, Syria, and Israel and Palestine form its southern, northern, and northern-eastern borders, respectively. There are a variety of landscapes throughout the nation, including lush plains, mountains, valleys, and deserts.

The western region of Jordan is dominated by the Jordan River Valley, a long, thin gully that runs the length of the country from north to south. The majority of Jordan's agriculture is concentrated in this area, which contains some of the most fertile land in the nation.

East of the Jordan River Valley on the Arabian Plateau is a region of rocky hills and mountains known as the eastern plateau. The stunning rock formations of Wadi Rum and the historic city of Petra are two of the eastern plateau's most notable features.

Jordan's climate is mostly hot and dry, with frigid winters and dry summers. In the summer, certain regions of the country may see temperatures as high as 40 degrees Celsius. Throughout the winter, temperatures hover around 10 degrees Celsius on average. The majority of the rainfall, which is mild and irregular, occurs between November and April.

In all, Jordan's topography and climate have a significant impact on the development of the nation's distinctive landscape, culture, and way of life.

CHAPTER TWO
PLANNING YOUR TRIP

WHEN TO GO

Jordan is a place that can be visited all year round, and every season has its own special attractions and activities to offer. When determining when to go, there are a few things to think about, such as the weather, people, and events.

The spring and autumn, from March to May and September to November, respectively, are the busiest travel seasons in Jordan. Temperatures in these months range from the low 60s to the mid 80s Fahrenheit, making for a comfortable and temperate climate. Many of the nation's festivals and cultural events also take place around this time, including the Jerash Festival of Culture and Arts, which involves performances in music, dance, and theater.

Jordan's summer, which lasts from June through August, may be very hot, with frequent highs of above 100 degrees Fahrenheit. The Aqaba Summer Festival, which features musical performances, sporting activities, and food markets, is one among the various festivals and events that take place at this time when many families have time off from work and school.

Jordan's winter, which lasts from December to February, may be quite cold, especially in the northern areas, where nighttime lows can reach the mid-30s F. Snowfall may lend a lovely touch to the environment, and this is also the time of year when the nation's natural landscapes are at their most lush and verdant. Additionally, at this time, people celebrate Christmas and New Year's, and towns like Amman and Madaba host several festivities.

The crowds should be taken into account while making travel plans to Jordan. Peak travel times may result in lengthy lineups and congested circumstances, especially at well-known destinations like Petra and Wadi Rum. Consider traveling during the shoulder seasons, when there are less visitors and more opportunity for quiet exploration, if you like a more laid-back and tranquil experience.

The ideal time to go to Jordan ultimately relies on your unique tastes and interests. Jordan offers lots to offer all year long, whether you're seeking for pleasant weather, cultural events, or a more sedate experience. So begin making travel arrangements right now and be ready to explore everything that this incredible nation has to offer.

How to Get There

There are various handy and quick ways to get to Jordan, depending on your location and interests. Here are a few of the most often used methods of travel to Jordan:

By air: Queen Alia International Airport, which is situated in Amman, the country's capital, is Jordan's primary international airport. Many significant international airlines, including Royal Jordanian, Emirates, Qatar Airways, and Turkish Airlines, use the airport as a hub. Many cities, including New

York, London, Paris, and Dubai, have direct flights to Amman. You may take a cab or shuttle bus from the airport to your hotel or other location after you arrive in Amman.

By Land: Israel, Palestine, Syria, Saudi Arabia, and Iraq all have borders with Jordan, allowing for access by land from these nations. The Allenby/King Hussein Bridge crossing from Israel to the city of Jericho is the busiest land border crossing. The Sheikh Hussein Bridge from Israel, which links to the city of Irbid, is another well-liked bridge.

By Water: Jordan is home to the little Red Sea port city of Aqaba. Although Aqaba does not have a regular passenger ferry service, it is nevertheless feasible to hire a private boat or yacht from neighboring nations like Egypt or Israel.

By Bus: A number of bus companies provide services between Jordan and its neighbors, notably Israel, Palestine, and Egypt. Additionally, the JETT bus operator runs frequent services from Amman to well-known locations within Jordan, such Petra and Aqaba.

By automobile: If you prefer to travel by automobile, you may enter Jordan from nearby nations. Before doing this, however, be cautious to verify the current state of safety and security, since certain border crossings could already be blocked or subject to limitations.

It's crucial to consider any visa requirements or travel limitations imposed as a result of the present state of the world's health while organizing your trip to Jordan. For the most recent information, be sure to check with your embassy or consulate. Before traveling, double-check that you have all the required paperwork and immunizations.

Getting Around

There are a few different ways to move about Jordan, depending on your interests and budget. Here are a few of the most often used transportation options in Jordan:

By Taxi: Taxis are a common means of transportation for visitors in Jordan and are extensively accessible across the country. They may be requested via your hotel or a taxi company, or they can be hailed on the street. Since meter usage is not always the case, take careful to haggle the price before entering the cab.

By Rental vehicle: Renting a vehicle makes it easy to discover Jordan since it offers you the flexibility to go off the beaten path and travel at your own leisure. Major cities like Amman have rental vehicle businesses, and airport pickup and drop-off arrangements may be made.

By Public transit: Buses and minibuses run all around Jordan, making it a pretty decent nation for public transit. Regular services connecting major towns and tourist hotspots like Petra and Aqaba are run by the JETT bus business.

By Private Tour: Take into account hiring a private tour guide or going on a group trip if you would like a more structured experience. This may be a useful approach to discover more about Jordan's history and culture and to see places that would be more challenging to get on your own.

By Bike: Cycling is a popular method to get in Jordan, especially in the Wadi Rum desert and along the King's Highway. In Amman and other cities, there are many places to hire bicycles, and guided riding trips are also offered.

It's vital to remember that driving may be difficult in Jordan, especially in crowded areas like Amman. If you do choose to hire a vehicle, be sure to educate yourself on local driving practices and traffic rules. Additionally, keep in mind that many cabs and buses do not take credit cards, so be sure to have enough of cash with you.

Visas and Documents

Before visiting Jordan, it is important to understand the documentation and visa requirements. You should be aware of the following:

Visas: The majority of travelers to Jordan need a visa, which may be obtained in advance or on arrival. Some nations, such as those from the United States, the United Kingdom, and Canada, may get visas upon arrival at Queen Alia International Airport in Amman or at specified land border crossings. It is best to call the Jordanian embassy or consulate nearest you to check the most updated visa requirements.

Documents:

In addition to a current passport and visa (if applicable), you should carry the following documents with you while visiting Jordan:

Travel Security: Even though it is not required, travel insurance is highly recommended for every trip to Jordan. It may offer coverage for medical expenses, travel delays or cancellations, and other unexpected events.

Evidence of Compromise: You may be asked to produce paperwork for your lodgings before entering Jordan. This may be a hotel reservation or a letter from a friend or family welcoming you.

If you wish to hire a car and drive in Jordan, you will need an international driving permit (IDP) in addition to a valid driver's license.

Health Records: Depending on where you are coming from and how you are feeling right now, you may be requested to submit records of specific vaccinations or medical conditions.

Before traveling to Jordan, be sure that all of your documents is up to date and valid. If the appropriate paperwork and visas are not produced, entry into the country may be denied.

Travel Insurance

Any trip, particularly one to Jordan, should include travel insurance. It may give peace of mind and monetary protection in the case of unplanned situations such as illness or accident, trip cancellation or interruption, or lost or stolen luggage. Keep the following in mind when considering getting travel insurance for your trip to Jordan:

Coverage Options:

There are various types of travel insurance to consider, including:

Medical coverage: This may cover any medical expenses incurred while traveling, including as emergency treatment, hospitalization, and medical evacuation.

Coverage for trip cancellation and interruption may assist you in recovering your non-refundable travel expenditures if you are forced to cancel or curtail your holiday due to an emergency such as illness or a natural disaster.

Baggage insurance may cover lost, stolen, or damaged baggage as well as personal belongings.

Coverage for emergency medical evacuation: If you get seriously ill or wounded while traveling, this may give coverage for an emergency medical evacuation.

Choosing a Service Provider:

Before choosing a travel insurance carrier, it is important to browse around and compare coverage options and rates. Choose a service provider with a good reputation and high customer satisfaction. If you plan to participate in adventure sports like hiking or diving while on vacation, it's important to know which providers provide specialized coverage for these activities.

Policy Considerations:

Before purchasing travel insurance, make sure you properly review the policy's terms and conditions. Take note of any exclusions or limits, such as those pertaining to pre-existing medical conditions or high-risk activities. It's also crucial to understand the claim-making procedure and any necessary supporting documentation.

Any trip, particularly one to Jordan, should include travel insurance. It may give financial security and peace of mind in the case of unanticipated situations.

When considering travel insurance be sure to evaluate available coverage choose a reputable provider and properly read the policy's terms and conditions. If you have enough insurance coverage, you may go to Jordan with more confidence and security.

Budgeting and Money

Money and finance are important considerations while arranging a trip to Jordan. The following information may assist you in making the most of your travel budget:

Jordan's national currency is the Jordanian dinar (JOD). It is advisable to exchange money at authorized exchange bureaus or banks to get the best rates. ATMs are now widely available in urban areas, and many hotels, restaurants, and businesses accept credit cards.

Budget: The cost of traveling in Jordan may vary depending on your travel choices, lodgings, and activities. Here are some fundamental spending guidelines to keep in mind:

Hostels and guesthouses with acceptable prices may be found for roughly 10 to 20 JOD per night. Luxury hotels may cost up to 100 JOD per night, while mid-range hotels and Airbnb rentals vary from 30 to 60 JOD.

Food: Meals at local restaurants and street sellers cost between 3 and 8 JOD. Meals costing between 10 and 30 JOD or more may be found in fine dining venues and western-themed restaurants.

Taxis and public transportation are inexpensive ways to get about town, with prices ranging between 1-3 JOD. Renting a car may be more expensive, with daily rates starting at roughly 30 to 40 JOD.

Admission to well-known tourist locations may range from 1 to 15 JOD, with guided tours and adventurous activities sometimes costing more.

Money-saving tips

Here are some suggestions for visiting Jordan on a budget:

- Instead of taking a taxi, use the bus or walk.
- Eat at local eateries and street vendors instead than expensive restaurants.
- Consider visiting major tourist locations during off-peak hours to avoid crowds and save money on entrance.
- Stay at a low-cost hotel or rent an Airbnb house.
- Haggling in local markets and shops is the best way to get the best discounts.

CHAPTER THREE
ACCOMONDATIONS OPTIONS

TYPES OF ACCOMMODATION

To accommodate the needs and preferences of every traveler, Jordan offers a broad selection of hotels. Here are a few of Jordan's most well-liked hotel options:

Hotels: Jordan has a vast range of hotels to choose from, ranging from affordable to opulent. Most hotels provide amenities including breakfast, Wi-Fi, and air conditioning.

Hostels: For travelers on a tight budget, hostels are a popular choice, particularly in major cities like Amman and Petra. Hostels provide dorm-style rooms with communal bathrooms and common areas.

Guesthouses: Guesthouses are a great option for those looking for a more authentic introduction to Jordanian culture. Guesthouses are often modest, family-run businesses that provide comfortable lodging with basic amenities.

Bed and Breakfasts (B&Bs) are a popular choice for tourists looking for a more individualized experience. Typically, B&Bs provide comfortable rooms with included breakfast.

In Jordan, camping is a popular pastime, particularly in arid regions like Wadi Rum. Some campsites provide more opulent facilities like private tents and en-suite bathrooms, while others just offer basic amenities like showers and toilets.

Eco-lodges: In Jordan, particularly in areas like the Dana Biosphere Reserve, eco-lodges are growing in popularity. Eco-lodges provide sustainable and environmentally friendly accommodation options, typically in picturesque and remote locations.

Many resorts may be found in Jordan, mostly in the port city of Aqaba. Facilities at resorts include restaurants, spas, and swimming pools.

Every traveler may choose a hotel in Jordan that suits their needs and preferences. Whether you're looking for inexpensive choices or opulent resorts, there are many options to suit every taste and budget.

Booking Recommendations

Making your travel arrangements in advance will enable you to save costs, reduce stress, and ensure a great vacation. Here are some ideas for organizing your Jordanian vacation:

Plan ahead: Jordan is a well-liked travel location, particularly during the summer. To get the best deals on flights, hotel, and activities, it is essential to plan your holiday well in advance.

Use online travel companies to find flights, accommodations, and activities. A few examples are Expedia, Booking.com, and Airbnb. Check prices and reviews to get the best deals.

Look for limited-time deals and discounts: On their websites or via third-party booking platforms, airlines, hotels, and tour operators often advertise deals and discounts. Sign up for email alerts or follow them on social media to be informed about the latest specials.

Think about taking a trip off-season: You may reduce the cost of your trip by traveling when it's off-peak. The off-season in Jordan lasts from November to March.

Organize your travel and lodging at the same time: When you book your travel and lodgings at the same time, many airlines and hotels offer discounts. This might help you save costs on your holiday.

Read the following evaluations before making a reservation: Check out traveler reviews before booking your lodgings or activities. This could enable you to stay safe from scams and enjoy your trip.

Reserve guided tours and activities in advance to ensure availability. If you wish to participate in guided tours or activities, you must reserve them in advance. Some well-liked Jordanian tours, like Petra by Night, need bookings in advance.

By planning beforehand, you may save money and guarantee a smooth and enjoyable trip to Jordan. You may acquire the best deals and have a stress-free trip by paying attention to these advices.

Recommendations for Accommodations

There are several hotel options available in Jordan for every style and price range. Here are some recommendations for places to stay in Jordan:

Marriott Amman: The Marriott Amman is a superb hotel that is situated in the heart of Amman. The hotel offers comfortable accommodations with amenities including a pool, Wi-Fi, and air conditioning. Those seeking a comfortable and opulent stay in Amman might consider staying at the Marriott Amman.

Petra Guest House: The Petra gate is only a short distance away from the Petra Guest House. The inn offers comfortable accommodations along with amenities like air conditioning, WiFi, and breakfast. For those who want to remain close to Petra and yet enjoy the stunning views of the surrounding mountains, the Petra Guest House is a fantastic choice.

Feynan Ecolodge Located in the Dana Biosphere. The ecolodge offers environmentally responsible hotel options with solar-powered hot water, electricity, and comfortable beds. For those who want to take advantage of Jordan's natural beauty while lessening their impact on the environment, the Feynan Ecolodge is a fantastic solution.

The Wadi Rum Night Luxury Camp is situated right in the middle of Wadi Rum. The camp offers luxurious tents with own patios, bathrooms with showers, and air conditioning. Those want to experience Wadi Rum's breathtaking desert landscape in luxury can choose the Wadi Rum Night Luxury Camp.

The Amman Pasha Hotel is a budget-friendly lodging option in the heart of Amman's city. The hotel offers comfortable accommodations along with amenities like air conditioning, WiFi, and breakfast. The Amman Pasha Hotel is a great choice for those on a tight budget who want to stay close to the city's top attractions.

umayyad palace in amman

CHAPTER FOUR
DESTINATION GUIDES

Amman

Amman, Jordan's capital, is a flourishing metropolis with a rich cultural past. Amman, often known as the "White City," is a city of contrasts in which historic and modern architecture types mix to create a unique urban landscape. Here's a basic breakdown of what to expect in Amman:

History and Culture:

Amman has a long history dating back to antiquity. A number of ancient structures and sites have been left in the city by several civilizations, including the Greeks, Romans, and Ottomans. Visitors may learn more about the city's rich history and culture by visiting the Roman Theater, Amman Citadel, and Jordan Archaeological Museum.

Amman is well-known for its excellent and diverse food scene. Visitors may try regional staples including hummus, falafel, and mansaf (a traditional lamb dish served with a yogurt sauce). There are also several cafés and tea shops where you may relax and drink some tea or coffee.

Shopping: Amman is a great place to go if you're seeking for traditional handicrafts like ceramics, rugs, and textiles. The city's markets, particularly the well-known souks in the centre of Amman, provide a wide range of goods at reasonable prices.

In Amman's thriving nightlife scene, there are several bars, clubs, and live music venues to choose from. Visitors may relax with a drink or dance the night away at one of the city's many entertainment venues.

Accommodations: Amman has a wide range of housing options to suit every taste and budget, from elegant hotels to low-cost hostels. Many of the hotels are ideally located near the city's major attractions and provide spectacular views of the skyline.

Top Attractions

Amman, Jordan's capital city, is a cultural, historical, and contemporary hub. This wonderful city is a fascinating site to see due to its peculiar combination of the antique and modern. The following are some of the most important sites in Amman that you should not miss:

The Roman Amphitheater, one of Amman's most iconic landmarks, dates back to the second century and is a spectacular sight to witness. This magnificent amphitheater, with 6,000 seats, is located in the heart of Amman's city. Climb to the peak for panoramic views of the city, and it is a popular venue for concerts and other cultural events.

Amman Citadel is a must-see attraction in Amman. It is positioned on a hill with a view of the city. Several civilizations, including the Greeks, Romans, and Ottomans, have called the citadel home since the Bronze Age. Tourists may visit the ancient city's relics such as the Archaeological Museum, the Umayyad Palace, and the Temple of Hercules.

The Jordan Museum is an innovative, interactive museum that celebrates Jordan's rich history and culture. The museum displays ancient Jordanian treasures such as the Dead Sea Scrolls as well as more modern history. The museum's wonderful café and outdoor garden are also available to visitors.

Rainbow Avenue: This bustling and busy boulevard in Amman is known for its stylish cafés, diners, and retailers. Visitors may take a leisurely stroll along the lively street, pausing to enjoy some excellent local cuisine or peruse the gift stores.

The Mosque of King Abdullah: The King Abdullah Mosque is one of Amman's most beautiful mosques and a must-see for visitors. This stunning mosque was built in 1989 and has a gorgeous blue dome, intricate tile work, and a huge prayer hall.

The Jordan National Gallery of Fine Arts is a spectacular museum that showcases the works of Jordanian and international artists. Because of its broad collection of works, including paintings, sculptures, and photos, the museum is an excellent place to learn about and appreciate art.

Hidden Germs

Even though Amman's major attractions are undeniably worth seeing, there are a few unknown gems that provide a unique and off-the-beaten-path experience. Here are a few hidden Amman attractions to consider:

The Abu Darwish Mosque is a beautiful mosque on a hill with views of the city. It is a tranquil and quiet setting away from the crowds, with stunning views of the city. Locals often come to pray at the mosque, which is named after a well-known Jordanian poet.

The Royal vehicle Museum is an intriguing museum that covers Jordan's vehicle history. The museum has vintage autos, motorcycles, and even tanks that have seen battle throughout Jordan's history. It's a terrific place to learn more about Jordan's automotive history and view some odd and collectable vehicles.

Amman's Jabal: This attractive Amman neighborhood is well-known for its stylish cafés, boutique businesses, and gorgeous historic residences. Visitors may wander around the packed streets and alleyways, appreciating the gorgeous architecture and the laid-back atmosphere.

Darat Al Funun: Darat Al Funun is a cultural center that hosts a range of events and activities such as lectures, concerts, and art exhibitions. The center, which is located in a charming old villa in the Jabal Al Weibdeh area, is an excellent place to learn about Jordanian culture and creativity.

The Wild Jordan Center is a unique eco-tourism site that offers a wide range of outdoor activities such as hiking, bird viewing, and nature tours. From its high perch above the city, the facility offers beautiful views of the surrounding countryside. The restaurant within the facility provides delicious regional cuisine produced with organic and locally sourced ingredients.

Recommendations for Food & Beverage

Jordanian cuisine is a combination of numerous cultures and cuisines, and Amman offers a diverse range of restaurants providing both traditional and modern fare. Here are some recommendations on things to eat and drink in Amman:

Mansaf: Mansaf is Jordan's national dish and something that everyone who visits the country must try. It is made out of rice and almonds, as well as lamb cooked in a yogurt sauce. Mansaf is offered in numerous Amman restaurants, although Sufra Restaurant and Al-Quds Restaurant are two of the finest.

Falafel: Falafel is a deep-fried Middle Eastern street food made of ground chickpeas and spices. Falafel may be found all across Amman, however Hashem Restaurant and Al-Quds Falafel are two of the best venues to try it.

Kunafa: Kunafa is a sweet and cheesy dish popular in Jordan and the Middle East. It's made with layers of shredded phyllo dough sandwiched between layers of cheese and topped with a sticky sweet sauce. There are several bakeries and sweet shops in Amman that sell kunafa, but Habibah Sweets and Al-Daya'a Sweet Shop are two of the best.

Coffee in Arabic: Arabic coffee is a popular beverage in Jordan and the Middle East. It's a strong, black coffee served in small cups with cardamom flavour. Arabic coffee is offered in many cafés in Amman, however Jafra Café and Hashem Restaurant are two of the best places to try it.

Fresh Juice: Fresh juice is a popular beverage in Amman, and there are several juice kiosks and companies across the city. Juice flavors that are often utilized include pomegranate, orange, and carrot. While fresh juice is accessible everywhere, Jabri Juice and Al-Quds Juice are two of the best places to try it.

Accommodation Recommendations

Amman has a wide variety of hotel alternatives to suit a variety of requirements and interests. Here are some hotel and hostel recommendations for your vacation to Amman, Jordan, ranging from five-star to budget-friendly:

The Four Seasons Hotel Amman is a luxurious hotel in the heart of the city. It has spacious rooms, a gym, a spa, and an outdoor pool. The hotel has a range of dining options, including restaurants from Italy and the Middle East.

Amman's Grand Millennium: The Grand Millennium Amman is a modern hotel located in the city's commercial district. It has a Japanese restaurant and a rooftop club, as well as well-appointed rooms, a fitness center, a rooftop pool, and a pool.

Amman Pasha Hotel: Located in the city's historic heart, the Amman Pasha Hotel provides an affordable overnight option. It has clean, comfortable rooms, a rooftop terrace with city views, and a restaurant offering traditional Jordanian cuisine.

Sydney Hotel: The Sydney Hotel is a boutique hotel located in the heart of the city. It offers comfortable rooms, a rooftop terrace with city views, and a restaurant offering Middle Eastern and international cuisine.

Jordan Tower Hotel: The Jordan Tower Hotel is a popular hostel located in the city's historic heart. It offers basic but clean rooms, access to a rooftop patio with city views, and a communal kitchen.

Arabic mosque amman

Petra

One of the most magnificent archaeological landmarks in the whole world is the ancient city of Petra, which is located in southwest Jordan. The unique rock-cut architecture of this beautiful city, which features elaborate temples, tombs, and amphitheaters carved directly into the pink sandstone cliffs, is well known.

Originally, the city served as the seat of the Nabataean Kingdom, a vast economic hegemony that controlled the trade routes between Arabia, Egypt, and Syria. The brilliant engineers and architects of the Nabataeans created an amazing complex of buildings and structures that still surprise visitors today.

The most well-known structure in Petra is The Treasury, which was carved into a sandstone rock and is estimated to have been constructed in the first century AD. The Nabataean rulers most likely used this beautiful building as a royal tomb or treasury. Among Petra's notable structures are the Monastery, the High Place of Sacrifice, and the Great Temple.

Along with its amazing architectural features, Petra is surrounded by stunning natural features including spectacular rock formations, deep valleys, and vast deserts. The fact that the city is tucked away in a valley with a narrow ravine called the Siq leading into it adds to the sense of mystery and wonder that visitors get while visiting this ancient city.

One of Jordan's most well-known tourist destinations is Petra, which is now a UNESCO World Heritage Site. People go here from all over the world to discover this beautiful city's rich history and culture. Petra is a city you shouldn't miss if you appreciate exploring new and intriguing places or if you are a history or architecture fan.

Top Attractions

Petra is a city of amazing beauty and wonder, with a wide variety of historic structures to discover and breath-taking natural surroundings. The following are some of the top Petra attractions you should not miss while there:

The Treasury: The Treasury is unquestionably Petra's most well-known structure and a must-see for tourists. This amazing building is carved out of a sandstone rock and decorated with intricate carvings and decorative elements. It is one of the most photographed buildings in the world and is said to have been built as a tomb or treasury for the Nabataean monarchs.

The Monastery is yet another amazing structure in Petra. It contains incredible architectural features including columns, arches, and intricate carvings, and it is also carved into a cliff. Visitors may get a sense of the spiritual and cultural richness of Petra's ancient past by visiting the Monastery, which is believed to have been a temple or other religious building.

The Siq is a narrow valley that enters Petra's heart. This amazing natural feature is surrounded by tall cliffs that reach heights of 80 meters, providing a dramatic and breath-taking entrance to the city. Along with several amazing rock inscriptions and formations, the Siq is home to numerous magnificent tombs and temples.

The Royal Tombs are a group of magnificent structures set high on a rock above Petra. These tombs have lovely carvings and decorations that can still be seen today. It is believed that they were built for Nabataean emperors and their families. One of the best places to take in Petra's stunning surroundings is at the Royal Tombs, which also provide visitors a chance to go back in time and experience the splendor and majesty of the Nabataean Kingdom.

The Great Temple is one of Petra's most impressive buildings and is said to have served as a significant religious site for the Nabataeans. Tall columns, a large courtyard, and exquisite carvings and decorations may still be seen in this temple today. For everyone interested in Petra's religious and cultural history, it is a must-see.

The High Place of Sacrifice is a rocky plateau that is situated far above Petra. The Nabataeans used this spectacular site for sacrifices and religious ceremonies, and now visitors may experience the spiritual and cultural significance of Petra's ancient past. The High Place of Sacrifice is renowned for its spectacular panoramic views of the landscape, which make it a prime spot for tourists and photography.

There are a lot more Petra's top sights to see; these are just a few. Whether you are interested in history, architecture, or the beauty of the natural world, Petra has something to offer everyone. So why not book your trip right now to experience the wonder and beauty of this magnificent medieval city for yourself?

Hidden Germs

While Petra has several well-known attractions like the Treasury and the Monastery, there are also some undiscovered gems that are worth exploring while you're there. Some of Petra's best-kept secrets are as follows:

The Garden Temple is a small temple in Petra that is hidden from view off the main path. It includes amazing carvings and decorations, a gorgeous garden, and a little pool. The Garden Temple is a stunning and serene spot perfect for a solitary stroll or a moment of meditation, despite not being as well-known as some of Petra's other attractions.

The Lion Monument is a modest monument that may be seen in a quiet area in Petra. It features a lovely lion and is said to have represented strength and power for the Nabataeans. The Lion Monument is a wonderful and fascinating piece of history that is worth visiting, even if it is not as gorgeous as some of Petra's other structures.

The Broken Pediment Tomb is a stunning structure that is situated high on a rock in Petra. Its odd architectural design and shattered pediment give the tomb a distinctive and striking appearance. The Broken Pediment Tomb is a marvel of ancient construction and design, and although getting there requires a little bit of hiking, the views from the top are just breathtaking.

Sextius Florentinus' Tomb, a largely unnoticed tomb in Petra, is called Sextius Florentinus' Tomb. It is believed to have been built for a wealthy Roman resident of Petra in the second century AD. It boasts a magnificent façade with intricate carvings and ornaments. The Tomb of Sextius Florentinus is an interesting and beautiful structure that is well worth viewing, despite not being as impressive as some of Petra's other tombs.

The Byzantine Church is a little church located in the heart of Petra. It has some impressive frescoes and embellishments and is estimated to have been built in the fifth or sixth century AD. Although small, the Byzantine Church is a fascinating and significant part of Petra's history and offers visitors a unique opportunity to experience the city's rich religious and cultural heritage.

These are only a few of Petra's undiscovered gems. While they may not be as well-known as some of the city's other sights, they provide visitors a chance to discover something fresh and unexpected while they're there as well as a unique and memorable way to engage with Petra's rich and fascinating past.

Recommendations for food and drink

A historical, cultural, and gastronomic treasure is Petra. Traditional Jordanian food and international cuisine are also available for consumption in Petra, providing visitors a wide range of options. The following are some of Petra's top restaurants and bars:

Mansaf: Mansaf is a traditional Jordanian dish that is revered as the nation's cuisine. It is made with lamb and served with bulgur or rice and a yogurt sauce. Mansaf is a hearty and delicious meal that is perfect for anybody who wants to experience the traditional flavors of Jordanian cuisine.

A well-known Middle Eastern delicacy called falafel is prepared from chickpeas or fava beans. It is often served in a pita bread with hummus, vegetables, and other sauces. Falafel is a healthy and delicious option for people looking for a vegetarian or vegan meal.

Kebabs: There are several restaurants and cafés in Petra that serve kebabs, a common street food in

Jordan. They are often perfectly grilled with marinated meat, such as lamb, beef, or chicken. Kebabs often come with rice, salad, and a selection of sauces and dips.

In Jordanian culture, Arabic coffee is a cornerstone and is often offered as a sign of welcome. It is often served in little cups with dates or other sweets and is a powerful and tasty coffee. Every tourist to Petra should drink Arabic coffee since it is such a significant part of the community there.

Another widely used beverage in Jordan is tea, which is often served with sugar and new mint leaves. It's a cool beverage that's perfect for a hot day in Petra and is offered at several eateries and cafés across the city.

A common Middle Eastern sandwich known as shawarma is made with marinated meat, usually chicken or beef, and is served in a pita with vegetables and a selection of sauces. For those who are always on the move and need a satisfying dinner to keep them going, shawarma is a quick and delectable option.

A common dip made with chickpeas, tahini, and other ingredients is called hummus. It is a pleasant and wholesome substitute that many Petra restaurants and cafés provide. It is great for dipping bread or vegetables.

Recommendations for Accommodations

There are many different housing options available to visitors to Petra, from pricey hotels to inexpensive hostels. Here are some lodging recommendations for your trip to Petra:

Mövenpick Resort Petra: The exquisite Mövenpick Resort Petra is located only a few meters from the historic site of Petra. Among the amenities offered by the hotel are a spa, a fitness facility, and a pool. The accommodations have spacious, cozy rooms with modern decor and all the comforts required for a peaceful stay.

Hotel Petra Moon: The Petra Moon Hotel is a mid-range lodging option that is situated in Petra's heart. The hotel has several amenities, including a restaurant, a rooftop patio, and rooms that are roomy and well-equipped. The hotel's location makes it a great place from which to explore the historic city of Petra.

Rocky Mountain Hotel: If you're looking for a cheap place to stay in Petra, consider the Rocky Mountain Hotel. The hotel offers straightforward yet tidy and comfortable accommodations close to the ancient city of Petra. In addition, the hotel has a restaurant and a rooftop terrace with stunning mountain views.

The Petra Guest House Hotel is yet another fantastic option for those looking for comfortable accomodation close to the Petra historic site. Among the amenities offered by the hotel are a restaurant, a pool, and a fitness center. The rooms are roomy and well furnished, and they have everything you need for a comfortable stay.

Staying at the Seven Wonders Bedouin Camp will provide you a unique and authentic experience. In the heart of the Wadi Rum desert, close to Petra, sits an eco-friendly resort. The camp offers accommodations in traditional Bedouin tents as well as a range of activities including camel rides and desert excursions.

Dead Sea

The Dead Sea is a distinctive and fascinating Jordanian city with its well-known saline lake and breathtaking natural beauty. Travelers to Jordan must see the Dead Sea, which is more than 400

meters below sea level and located at the lowest place on Earth.

The Dead Sea is well known for its salt lake, which is around 10 times saltier than the ocean and is so salty that fish cannot survive there. Attributable to the water's exceptional buoyancy, which is also attributable to the high salt content, visitors, may float freely on the lake's surface.

In addition to its well-known salty lake, the Dead Sea is surrounded by stunning desert scenery and uninhabited mountains, making it a favorite hiking and outdoor sports destination. One of the world's oldest continuously inhabited towns, the ancient city of Jericho is only one of the many archeological sites nearby that tourists may explore.

Many travelers go there to benefit from the saltwater and mineral-rich mud of the Dead Sea, which is well-known for its therapeutic benefits. There are numerous opulent spas and wellness centers nearby that provide a variety of therapies and treatments to aid tourists in unwinding and reviving.

Every visitor to Jordan should visit the Dead Sea whether they want to take in the area's natural beauty, learn about its distinct cultural legacy, or just unwind and rest.

Top Attractions

Due to its unusual geographic position and health advantages, Jordan is home to the Dead Sea, the lowest spot on Earth. The region's beautiful landscapes, natural marvels, and historic sites draw visitors from all over the globe.

In the area, the Dead Sea itself is a well-liked tourist destination. This salty lake's notoriously high salt content makes swimming there a unique experience. The "Dead Sea" received its name because of the extreme salt concentration in the water, which makes it impossible for any living thing to exist there. As a result of the lake's famed therapeutic benefits, people seeking treatment for skin and respiratory diseases often go there.

There are several biblical and historical locations close to the Dead Sea. One of the oldest continuously inhabited settlements in the world is the ancient city of Jericho, which lies only a few kilometers from the Dead Sea. The area has an 8000 BC archaeological site, and it is thought that people have lived there constantly ever since. Discover the history and culture of the ancient city of Jericho by exploring its ruins.

The Baptism Site, where John the Baptist is said to have baptized Jesus, is another well-liked destination in the Dead Sea region. Numerous Christian tourists from throughout the globe visit this sacred location to take in the spiritual ambiance.

Anyone who appreciates the outdoors must visit the Ein Gedi Nature Reserve. There are several freshwater springs, waterfalls, and ponds in this natural reserve. Swim in the pools, explore the reserve's lovely pathways, and savor the breathtaking views of the mountains and surrounding areas.

Additionally, the Dead Sea region is widely renowned for its opulent resorts that let visitors unwind and rest in style. These resorts provide amenities like spas, swimming pools, and excellent dining options, making for a pleasant holiday experience.

Hidden Germs

Despite the Dead Sea's well-known health advantages, there are several undiscovered sights that travelers may discover while visiting. Some of the Dead Sea's best-kept secrets are listed below:

A magnificent canyon may be found close to the Dead Sea in Wadi Mujib. It is a well-liked hiking location with lovely views of the surroundings.

According to biblical narrative, Lot and his family hid in this cave as Sodom and Gomorrah were being destroyed. The cave is accessible through a short trek and is situated on the Dead Sea's eastern edge.

About an hour's drive from the Dead Sea lies the ancient fortress known as Al Karak, which dates to the Crusader era. It offers a window into Jordan's colorful past and is a must-see for history aficionados.

A popular spot for relaxation and rejuvenation is Ma'in Hot Springs. The Dead Sea is around 30 kilometers distant from them. After a long day of touring, the hot springs are an excellent spot to relax and are said to offer therapeutic benefits.

Approximately two hours from the Dead Sea, the Dana Biosphere Reserve is home to a wide variety of flora and animals. Both guided tours and just admiring the area's natural beauty are available to visitors.

The Mukawir Fortress, a historic fortress perched above the Dead Sea, is where John the Baptist is claimed to have been killed. It is a must-see for everyone interested in history and architecture and gives breathtaking views of the region.

John the Baptist is credited with baptizing Jesus in Bethany Beyond the Jordan. The location, which has historic churches and baptizing waters, is a well-liked Christian pilgrimage attraction.

Visitors to Jordan are likely to enjoy a fulfilling and memorable experience because of the abundance of undiscovered gems in the Dead Sea region.

Recommendations for food and drink

The Bedouin, Mediterranean, and Middle Eastern influences on the regional cuisine of Jordan's Dead Sea area are well recognized. The dish is simple yet tasty, and it is spiced up with a variety of herbs and seasonings.

One of the most well-known foods in the area is mansaf, a lamb or chicken entree prepared in the bedouin manner that is served with rice and a sour sauce made of yogurt. Musakhan, a classic Palestinian meal made with roasted chicken, onions, and sumac and served on flatbread, is another preferred option.

There are several delectable sweets available in Jordan, including baklava, a sweet pastry consisting of layers of phyllo dough filled with chopped nuts and honey, and kunafa, a pastry filled with sweet cheese and drizzled with syrup.

The Dead Sea area has a variety of foreign eating alternatives, including Italian, Indian, and American food, in addition to traditional Jordanian cuisine.

Enjoy a range of cool drinks while touring the Dead Sea area, including mint tea, Arabic coffee, and fresh fruit juices. Jordan is recognized for producing top-notch wines, and many nearby vineyards provide wine tasting events.

Recommendations for Accommodations

The Dead Sea in Jordan is a well-liked vacation spot recognized for its salty lake, mineral-rich mud, and all-natural therapeutic properties. Visitors swarm to this location to take in the natural marvels of the area, renew their skin, and treat illnesses. The Kempinski Hotel Ishtar is one of the greatest hotels in Dead Sea, and visitors may choose from a variety of lodging choices, from opulent resorts to more affordable alternatives. The resort is renowned for its opulent amenities and breath-taking Dead Sea vistas. There are 345 bedrooms, suites, and villas total, each with its own patio or balcony. The hotel offers a variety of dining options, a spa, nine swimming pools, and a private beach.

The Movenpick Resort & Spa Dead Sea is another well-liked choice. The 346 rooms and suites of the resort provide breathtaking views of the Dead Sea. It has many swimming pools, one of which is an infinity pool, a private beach, a spa, and a selection of dining options.

The Dead Sea Spa Hotel is a great choice for individuals on a tight budget. The hotel has 265 rooms, a private beach, a pool, a spa, and a number of dining options. In addition, a range of sports, including horseback riding, cycling, and hiking, are available at the hotel.

The Crowne Plaza Jordan Dead Sea Resort & Spa is another affordable alternative with breathtaking views of the Dead Sea. There are 420 rooms, suites, and villas in the hotel, each having an own patio or balcony. The hotel has a number of swimming pools, a private beach, a fitness facility, a spa, and a variety of eating establishments.

The Dead Sea offers a range of lodging choices, whether visitors are searching for opulent or affordable lodging. Every visitor to Jordan should see the Dead Sea because of its amazing beauty and all-natural therapeutic abilities.

Jericho cityscape

CHAPTER FIVE
ACTIVITIES AND EXPERIENCES

Adventure Sports

Jordan offers a diverse choice of adrenaline-pumping adventure activities. Here are some of the top Jordan adventure activities to do, ranging from desert walks to Red Sea scuba diving:

Adventure activities accessible in Wadi Mujib, a natural environment near the Dead Sea, include canyoning, trekking, and rock climbing. One of the most popular activities is wading across a short canyon with waist-deep water on the Siq Trail.

Wadi Rum: This desert valley is noted for its stunning rock formations and scarlet sand dunes. Adventure activities like as rock climbing, trekking, and camel riding are accessible in Wadi Rum. One of the most popular activities is a 4x4 Jeep journey into the desert to see some of the most breathtaking vistas.

Aqaba: This Red Sea port city is popular for snorkeling and scuba diving. The crystal-clear waters of the Red Sea are home to a diverse range of marine life, including bright coral reefs and unique species. Other exciting activities accessible in Aqaba include paragliding, windsurfing, and jet skiing.

The Dana Biosphere Reserve offers a variety of hiking and trekking paths for outdoor lovers. The reserve has a range of geographic features, including woodlands, mountains, and canyons. One of the most well-known climbs is the Dana to Petra route, which leads you through stunning desert landscapes to the ancient city of Petra.

The northern Ajloun Forest Reserve in Jordan is a natural reserve that offers a variety of hiking and trekking options. The reserve is home to dense forests, waterfalls, and stunning mountain views. One of the most popular hikes is the Soapmaker's Trail, which takes you through magnificent forests and old soap-making facilities.

Cultural Activities

Jordan is a country with a rich cultural history that provides several possibilities for visitors to thoroughly immerse themselves in the local way of life. The following are some of Jordan's top cultural activities:

Visit Historic Sites: Jordan's numerous historical sites include the famed city of Petra, the Roman city of Jerash, and the medieval castle of Karak. By visiting these sites, you may learn more about the country's interesting past and marvel at the incredible architectural and technical feats of prior civilizations.

Explore Bedouin Culture: Bedouins are nomadic people that have long lived in Jordan. Consider visiting a Bedouin camp to learn about their culture and enjoy their hospitality, which involves sipping sweet tea and eating Zarb, an underground-cooked cuisine.

Learning some simple Arabic words is the greatest approach to engage with people and extend your cultural experience. Jordan's official language is Arabic. Consider taking a class or hiring a tutor to learn the language.

Try Jordanian cuisine: Jordanian cuisine is a wonderful blend of Mediterranean and Middle Eastern flavors. Mansaf, a traditional Jordanian dish of lamb cooked in a yogurt sauce, and falafel, a popular vegetarian street snack, are two must-try meals.

Participate in a Cultural Festival: Jordan has a variety of cultural events throughout the year that promote the country's music, dance, and artwork. Among the most well-known events are the Jerash

Festival of Culture and Arts, the Amman International Film Festival, and the Petra International Music Festival.

Museum visits: Jordan has a variety of museums that exhibit the country's history and culture. Among the top museums to visit are the Petra Archaeological Museum, the Jordan Folklore Museum, and the Jordan Museum in Amman.

Food and Beverages

Jordan has a rich culinary legacy that has been influenced by its neighbors' tastes and cooking techniques, particularly Syria, Lebanon, and Palestine. Fresh herbs, spices, olive oil, and grilled meats are often employed in the country's diverse cuisine. Jordan provides a wide range of dining options to suit all tastes and budgets, from street food to high-end restaurants.

Mansaf's traditional meal is a gastronomic experience you must enjoy while in Jordan. Jordan's national dish, mansaf, is often prepared for special occasions such as weddings, funerals, and religious festivals. This meal is a wonderful combination of delicate lamb or chicken cooked in a rich and creamy sauce made from fermented dry yogurt, served over a bed of fluffy rice and topped with toasted almonds and pine nuts.

Falafel is another Jordanian delicacy that should not be overlooked. These crispy chickpea fritters are a popular street food in Jordan and are offered by a variety of vendors around the country. Because they are often served with tahini sauce, tomatoes, pickles, and fresh herbs, they are a pleasant and healthful snack.

If you want a really unique gourmet experience, you should try Bedouin cuisine. In a Bedouin-style dining setting, diners are served a traditional meal of roasted meat, fresh salads, and sweet tea while reclining on carpets and cushions and bathed in candlelight. This event is unique and intriguing since it often includes live music and narration.

Jordan's coffee culture, which is well-known across the globe, is an important part of its social and cultural traditions. Cardamom is often added in the coffee brewing process, resulting in a delicious and fragrant beverage.

In addition to traditional Jordanian cuisine, Jordan offers a range of international eating options. For those seeking a more upscale dining experience, there are various high-end restaurants located around the country that provide fusion meals of Mediterranean, Middle Eastern, and other cuisine.

Experiences with Wildlife and Nature

Jordan offers a diverse range of ecosystems and landscapes, giving visitors several opportunity to explore the natural world and wildlife. From the steep highlands of Wadi Rum to the verdant plains of the Jordan Rift Valley, there are several opportunities to explore and immerse oneself in Jordan's natural grandeur.

The Dana Biosphere Reserve, located in southern Jordan, is one of the greatest sites to see nature. This reserve encompasses more than 300 square kilometers of rocky mountains, gorges, and valleys and is home to a diverse range of flora and animals, including some rare and endangered species. Visitors may meander about the reserve, go on guided nature excursions, or go on a wildlife safari to see the natural fauna, which includes wolves, foxes, ibexes, and various bird species.

Another must-see natural wonder in Jordan is the Dead Sea. Despite the fact that it is technically a lake, the Dead Sea is one of the world's most well-known natural wonders owing to its unique properties. Because the waters are so salty and mineral-rich, swimmers may float freely in them, and the mud in the region is said to have skin-healing properties. Tourists may have a mud bath at one of the many spas and resorts located around the Dead Sea's shoreline.

Everyone who appreciates bird watching should go to the Azraq Wetland Reserve. This oasis in Jordan's eastern desert attracts migratory species such as flamingos, storks, and eagles. Visitors may explore the region on their own or with the assistance of a guide.

Finally, every trip to Jordan should include a stop in Wadi Rum. This stunning desert area is home to Bedouin people that have lived there for millennia, in addition to various remarkable rock formations and canyons. Visitors may sleep under the stars, experience Bedouin hospitality, and take guided vehicle tours or camel rides into the desert.

Festivals and Special Events

Jordan's vibrant culture is on show all year via a variety of festivals and events. Jordan is a nation rich in both old traditions and modern wonders. There is always a cause to rejoice in Jordan, whether it be via cuisine, music, or dance.

One of the most well-known events is the Jerash Festival, which takes place every year in July in the medieval city of Jerash. This worldwide cultural extravaganza brings together musicians, actors, and performers from all over the world to showcase their talents in a variety of traditional and modern styles. Visitors may enjoy live music, dancing performances, and theatrical presentations in the stunning backdrop of the ancient Roman ruins.

Another popular event is the Al-Balad Music Festival, which takes place in Amman throughout the summer. This event features a wide range of musical genres, from current pop and rock to traditional Jordanian music. It also provides lectures and seminars on music and culture, providing tourists with an in-depth look at the country's rich cultural past.

For those interested in religious holidays, the Mawlid Al-Nabi festival, which commemorates the Prophet Muhammad's (S.A.W) birthday, is a prominent event in the Islamic calendar. Visitors may attend parades, musical performances, and other activities commemorating the Prophet's life and teachings.

The annual Jordan Food Week, which takes place in Amman and other cities around the country, is a culinary feast. At this gourmet festival of Jordanian cuisine, visitors may experience a range of traditional Jordanian dishes as well as modern fusion food created by some of the country's greatest chefs.

Other notable events include the Red Sea Jazz Festival, held annually in Aqaba, and the Petra International Music Festival, held in the ancient city of Petra. These events bring together performers and music aficionados from across the world while exhibiting the best of Jordanian and worldwide music.

CHAPTER SIX
PRACTICAL INFORMATION

Health and Safety

Health and safety are always top priorities while traveling, and this is no different in Jordan. Here are some suggestions and tools to make your travel safe and enjoyable:

Immunizations: Before visiting Jordan, it is advised that you obtain the flu shot, as well as up-to-date vaccines for common illnesses including measles, mumps, and rubella. You could also need typhoid, hepatitis A, and hepatitis B vaccinations, depending on your schedule.

Food and Water Safety: Be cautious while consuming meals and liquids. Stay away from adding ice cubes to your drinks and always use bottled or filtered water. Make sure the food has been fully cooked before consuming any street food. Avoiding eating raw or undercooked meat and seafood is also suggested.

Jordan is a sunny country, thus it's important to protect yourself from the sun's harmful rays. Apply sunscreen with a minimum SPF of 30 and reapply every few hours. When it's hot out, wear a hat, some sunglasses, and look for cover.

Since Jordan is a conservative country, visitors should observe local customs and dress modestly, especially while visiting sacred sites. Women should wear comfortable clothing that covers their arms, legs, and heads. In certain areas, a headscarf may also be required.

Jordan is a largely safe country, although taking precautions against crime is always a good idea. A secure location should be used to store valuables such wallets, passports, and electronic gadgets. Pickpockets should be avoided in crowded areas. When traveling alone at night, stay in populated, well-lit areas.

Call the Jordanian police at 191 or 911 in case of an emergency. Although Jordan's hospitals and medical facilities are often of the highest caliber, those without travel insurance may find that receiving medical attention is expensive.

Although Jordan is generally a safe and stable country, it is important to be aware of the political climate, especially when traveling close to the borders. Check with your government for any travel advisories or warnings before you go.

Internet and Communication

Every journey to a new place requires communication and connection, and Jordan is no exception. Being a modern country, Jordan offers a wide range of communication options, from traditional phone services to cutting-edge mobile technology and high-speed internet.

For those who must stay connected while traveling, Jordan offers a strong mobile network. Three major mobile service providers are present in the country: Zain, Orange, and Umniah. Prepaid and postpaid SIM cards, as well as a range of plans for local and international calls and data use, are all offered by these companies.

Additionally, Jordan has a top-notch internet infrastructure, and the majority of its hotels, cafes, and restaurants provide free Wi-Fi to its patrons. Larger cities and towns have a large number of internet cafes for those who need high-speed internet.

There are several public telephones spread out around the country that provide traditional phone services and may be used with coins or prepaid cards. International calls may also be made using these pay phones. Additionally, a lot of hotels and coffee shops have landlines that may be used to make both local and international calls.

Mail may be sent both domestically and abroad through Jordan's rapid and reliable national postal service. There are other courier services available throughout the country for time-sensitive or important documents.

Etiquette and regional traditions

Visitors should respect local customs and etiquette since Jordan is a country with a rich history and culture. The following advice can assist you in comprehending Jordanian culture:

Modest attire Jordan is a conservative country, therefore wearing appropriately is crucial, especially when visiting places of worship. It is recommended to wear clothing that covers your shoulders, knees, and waist and to stay away from wearing anything too tight or exposed.

Take off your shoes when entering a mosque or someone's home, it is customary to take your shoes off. Additionally, it's usual to knock and wait for the host to open the door for you.

Use your right hand: In Jordan, it is important to eat, drink, and offer things to others with your right hand since the left hand is seen as unclean.

Esteeming seniors Respect for older people is highly valued in Jordanian culture. It is important to use formal titles, such as "Hajj" for men and "Hajja" for women, when speaking to someone elder or in a position of authority.

Shaking hands and exchanging pleasantries are customary when meeting someone for the first time. It's also polite to ask how their family and health are doing.

Public displays of love: In Jordanian culture, public displays of love are unusual and sometimes frowned upon.

Ramadan: During the holy month of Ramadan, Muslims fast from sunrise till dusk. By refraining from eating, drinking, or smoking in public during daytime hours, you may honor those who are fasting.

Jordan does not have a tipping culture, yet it is respected. Even though there may be a 10% service charge added to the bill in restaurants, it is still usual to leave a little tip for very good service.

If you adhere to these customs and respect Jordanian culture, your trip to the country may be more enjoyable and fulfilling.

Language Guide

Modern Standard Arabic is the official language of Jordan, which is mostly an Arabic-speaking country. In contrast, English is widely spoken and understood in most major cities, particularly in the tourist industry.

Here are a few common Arabic phrases along with their English translations:

Hello: Marhaba

Goodbye: Ma'a salama

Thank you: Shukran

Please: Min fadlak (to a man) / Min fadlik (to a woman)

Yes: Na'am

No: La

Excuse me: 'Afwan

Sorry: Asif

It's a good idea to get familiar with a few basic words in the native tongue before traveling to any foreign nation. You may use it to order meals, ask for directions, and haggle at marketplaces.

If you want to go to more rural or isolated places, learning some fundamental Jordanian Arabic phrases may be necessary since regional dialects differ substantially from Modern Standard Arabic. There are a few Bedouin tribes in Jordan who speak their own distinctive dialects.

Package Make a list of comfortable, breathable attire. Jordan may become rather warm, particularly in the summer, so bring lightweight, breathable clothes made of natural fibers like cotton or linen. It is essential to wear modest clothing, particularly while visiting places of worship.

shoes that are comfy for walking Since you'll be walking a lot in Jordan, pack some comfy walking shoes or sneakers.

Providing sun protection Use sunscreen, a hat, and sunglasses to shield your eyes from the piercing sun. Bring high SPF sunscreen, and reapply often.

Water bottle: In Jordan, it's important to stay hydrated, so pack a lightweight, refillable water bottle.

When entering mosques or other places of worship, women must wear a scarf or shawl to cover their heads and shoulders. A scarf or shawl could be useful.

Bring a swimsuit if you want to explore the Dead Sea or any of Jordan's other aquatic attractions.

When visiting Jordan, keep in mind to bring your camera or smartphone since the country is a photographer's dream.

Jordan only takes plugs of type C, D, F, and G, therefore bring a power adaptor if you are coming from a nation that employs a different kind.

Medication: Don't forget to pack any required medicines, including prescription drugs and over-the-counter treatments for common conditions.

Although credit cards and cash are both accepted in Jordan, it's always a good idea to carry extra cash about just in case.

Travel security: Before visiting Jordan, think about getting travel insurance to cover medical emergencies, trip cancellations, and other unforeseen events.

Portable energy supply: Use a portable charger to keep your electronics charged while you're on the go.

Compact backpack when going on day travels, a small bag may come in helpful for carrying goods.

Bring the necessities, like shampoo, conditioner, toothpaste, and any other personal care products you may need.

First aid equipment: A simple first aid kit including bandages, antiseptic cream, and painkillers may be useful while traveling.

Conclusion

A distinctive fusion of history, culture, and scenic beauty can be found in Jordan. There are several chances for adventure, discovery, and leisure, from the ancient city of Petra to the breathtaking landscapes of Wadi Rum.

While traveling to Jordan, it is important to keep in mind the nation's health and safety regulations as well as its traditions and manners. There may be obstacles in the way of connection and communication, but they may be overcome.

You must prepare ahead of time and pack sensibly if you want your vacation to go well and be fun. This entails taking into account the weather, the activities that are scheduled, and any cultural conventions.

Finally, we must adopt sustainable travel practices as responsible tourists by using less plastic, supporting local companies, and protecting the environment.

Traveling sustainably:

Instead of buying disposable water bottles, bring your own, and support regional vendors and artists by buying your meals and gifts from small stores and marketplaces.

Respect the environment by keeping natural areas clean and undamaged.

Consider using the bus, walking, or cycling as alternatives to renting a vehicle.

Pay attention to how much power and water are used in hotels and public spaces.

Printed in Great Britain
by Amazon